Encore

A Collection of Verse & Song Poems

2nd Edition

Marjorie E. "Marge" Potter

Encore

A Collection of Verse & Song Poems

by Marjorie E. "Marge" Potter

Copyright © 2018
by Marjorie E. Potter

Cover Design by Elizabeth Hauff

2nd Printing

ISBN — 9781626130975

Library of Congress Control Number — 2018954865

Published by ATBOSH Media ltd.

Cleveland, Ohio, USA

http://www.atbosh.com

Introduction:
A Note To The Reader

Before you select any poem, please read the two verses **"Preface"** & **"Dedication"** first.

The selections herein are largely autobiographical, although, as stated in "Preface", 'I take license with facts to promote the Rhyme'.

Once you read my work, you will come to know me somewhat — for the writings chronicle some major events in my life.

In general, I have kept them in chronological order. However, "Preface" and "Dedication" which are the first two poems in this edition, were not my first verses; rather, were written after many of the others.

In August 2000, I was invited to the International Society of Poetry Convention in Washington, D.C., where I competed with approximately 4,000 Poet/Artists from all over the world, and was inducted into the Society as a Poet of Merit.

My Title Poem, "Encore", was selected as one of the 200 Semi-Finalists. I was amazed and pleased beyond measure. The poem, written in 1974, came back to 'haunt' me, inspire me, if you will, to plunge ahead and self-publish my work. I had always wanted to publish, mainly as a gift to my children, for the great happiness they have brought to our lives.

I say 'our' lives, because their father, Johnny God bless him, had the soul of an Artist, too, but could never express himself as he wished he could. Perhaps he too, speaks to them now through my labor of love. He died on September 6, 1993.

Author's Dedication

The true 'Dedication' is to Johnny and my Family.

My thanks to the many friends who helped me along the way, in untold ways; to my dear friend, Bill Kribbs, Printer, Publisher, who put the first edition of this book together; to my publisher of this second edition, Jared Bendis; to Elizabeth Hauff who designed the cover for this edition; to my daughter Karen for encouraging me to publish the second edition and to her husband, Gary and her for overseeing the project; to the people I met on a train trip from D.C. to Connecticut, and Connecticut to Upstate New York the summer before the first printing; to the very special lady in the diner car on the train, Maureen Mahoney, who plied me with hot coffee and hot chocolate so that she could hear me read some of my poems. What a compliment! And, thanks to Mimsey from Rome, who loved them too.

Both of these ladies were an inspiration to me, and the first two copies of my first edition, were sent to them.

Thanks, also to my dear friend, Ada, who talked to me into the midnight hours the night before the competition and helped me to select the 'right' poem to 'read' at my appointed hour.

Thanks too, to Tony and Maria and Anthony, Jr. and Jessica, for making me feel completely loved as a member of their extended family; to Anne and Tom, owners of the beautiful Bed and Breakfast Inn, Antiques and Accommodations, in North Stonington, Connecticut, where I stayed, all too briefly, for their gracious hospitality and generosity; and to Laurie and Colleen at the Watermark, also in North Stonington, Connecticut who kindly invited me to give a 'reading' and share my work.

Thanks again to all of you. My life is richer because of you! Words are scarcely adequate for me to express my deepest heartfelt thanks to you all! You all are my life! In the words of my "Dedication":

'Without your love, there just wouldn't be

Much reason for living and being for me'.

Marjorie E. Potter, Summer 2018

Table of Contents

Introduction - A Note To The Reader	5
Author's Dedication	7
Table of Contents	9
Preface	11
Dedication	12
Remember When	13
Who Am I?	15
Lament	16
A Mother's Prayer	18
A Rose	21
With Us	22
The Voice Within	23
Lust	25
The Doers' Society	27
Legacy To My Children (And Others)	30
I Know	33
Musing—On New London	35
To A Friend	37
To Anne	39
Spirit Conversation	41
My Mailbox	42
To Cathy And Mary	43
My Son	45
It's Just A Thought Away	47

The Transition	48
Life Begins At Forty	50
Revolt	51
Lord, Help Me!	52
Touching	53
Encore	55
The Poll	57
Thoughts On New Year's Eve, '75	59
Feelings	60
Another Life	61
The Sea	65
My Place	66
Dear Eddie:	67
Miss You	69
Miss You (The Song)	71
If A Thief You Be	73
To My First Love	74
Time	76
When I Grow Old	77
Words	79
Wouldn't You?	81
If We Could But See Tomorrow	82
Forgiveness	83
About The Author	85

Preface

As poets have done since the beginning of time,
I take license with facts to promote the rhyme;

But, surely you'll get the main idea
And not look upon this as a panacea

But, rather, a diversion, momentary,
As you read this, my commentary

On various subjects as old as time
And some answers I found as I wrote the rhyme.

Marjorie E. Potter
February 29, 1972

Dedication

It's the poets who've said, as I recall,
That "Into each life, some rain must fall"

And, I admit, I've had my share,
And, thought it sometimes too much to bear

But, I've managed somehow to take it in tow
And, learn from it, the things I must know.

Don't think me an angel, nor a super-wit
I'm just now 'getting the hang of it'.

And, I think, from now on, I'd like to spend
The time in life that I can lend

In helping others in time of need
Lending a hand with some kind deed.

For this I know, beyond a doubt,
Many others have helped me out.

And this book is a 'thank you', to all who've
    shared
A part of my life, because you cared.

Without your love, there just wouldn't be
Much reason for living, and being, for me.

                                Marjorie E. Potter
                                    May 2, 1973

Remember When

Remember When
You really felt affinity for someone.

Remember when,
You really knew you understood.

Recall a time,
When someone said, "I love you";

And, time stood still!

The earth was fresh - -
The air so sweet - -

The sun, in all its radiance,
Bathed your love.

The breaking surf
Ebbed back to sea - -

To flow again,
Throughout Infinity.

Relive again,
The wondrous, magic feeling of the moment - -

And, know again,
Your love was really understood.

Recall, again,
When someone said, "I love you";

And, Time Stands Still.

Marjorie E. Potter
1969

Who Am I?

Devil, angel, witch, or saint!
I've heard them all—with some, complaint.
I'm each of these, alternately,
But, none for keeps, fortunately.

I've been before, and will again,
Be all the things I've ever been.
The sum of all I've been before,
Is in me now; and, there's yet more

Whatever's been added this time around,
Whoever I am, I am, I've found!

The devil, the angel, the witch, and the saint
Dwell within me, under restraint;

And, which of these I choose to be,
The choice is mine....I am! I'm free!

Marjorie E. Potter
March 10, 1970

Lament

What's the good of virtue
When your lover is in doubt?
Why would he try to hurt you?
What's the world all about?

When you've truly, deeply loved him
And you've given him your life
Borne him children who adore him;
And, to him you've been a 'wife'.

What's the reason for existence
When you feel it's all for naught?
Can you tolerate the pretense
When you feel you've just been 'bought'?

You're the 'tinsel' on the package of his life.
You're what it takes to fit the 'picture'—
You're his wife.
You may not always do your job well,
But your conscience lets you sleep well,
And, that's the secret of a long and healthy life.

So, that's the good of virtue
When your lover is in doubt.
No matter how he hurts you—
That's what life is all about.

You're the 'tinsel' on the package of his life.
You're what it takes to fit the 'picture'—
You're his wife.
You may not always do your job well,
But your conscience lets you sleep well;
And, that's the secret of a long and healthy life.

Marjorie E. Potter
May 11, 1970

A Mother's Prayer

Lord in Heaven, God of all,
Go behind the prison wall…

Seek the Warden, there you'll find—
Make him have a change of mind.

By Old "Bear Cat", he is known,
Fear and hatred has he sewn.

Gone unnoticed his evil deeds
But by those who cannot heed

Lest they lose body and soul
While imprisoned in that 'hole'—

Subject to his evil whim,
They must fear for life and limb.

Bring down grief upon his heart
For deeds in which he's played a part—

With the speed of light and claps of thunder,
Let his heart be torn asunder.

Make it last, lest he forget—
Instill Your will while he suffers yet.

Yes, I know, saith the Lord, "Vengeance is Mine"—
But, hear me out, read every line.

Rapid changes must he make—
Rules he's made, he must break.

Let his guiding Light be LOVE—
So none can stop him, from above.

Let his Unit's record show,
That only love can make men grow.

Through love, he'll order: "On Christmas Day,
All who want to visit may!"

And, to those, who think he's deranged—
Smiling, he'll say: "Things have changed!

"Let no man here doubt my word,
"My rules in the past have been absurd.

"In recent days, I've seen 'The Light'—
"Love is the rule, Men. No more might!

"Each man here, in our care,
"Has a burden that we share—

"Are we not as guilty as he
"If we don't help to make him 'free'?

"No men are Masters, no men Slaves;
"For, each, above all, his freedom craves.

"Give each his dignity, each, his soul—
"Let each one have his earthly 'role'...

"Then, of us, let it be said,
"This was no place of living dead;

"But, rather, a place where each did his part,
"To give his 'brother' peace in his heart;

"And, as we bid 'Farewell', to a departing 'brother',
"And, in his place, we greet another,

"Let us again renew our aim—
"In the goodness of man, we stake our claim;

"And, we'll lay down our lives, if need must be,
To make another 'brother' free!"

Then, O' God, in your Wisdom, all seeing,
Reward the Warden with his new 'being',

Free from grief and pain and sorrow—
Unless he forgets on some new tomorrow,

The progress and the changes wrought,
While Your will, not his, he sought.

And, thank you now, for my dear son,
And all the others, every one.

Marjorie E. Potter
November 30, 1970

A Rose

In Huntsville town beyond 'the wall',
A 'rose' still blooms, so proud and tall;

And, changing though the seasons are,
That 'rose' remains, without a scar.

'Twas planted there way last June—
Transplanted here, it will be soon.

Though slightly wilted it may be
Before it's sent back home to me,

When it is placed in that garden of mine,
To stand beside a 'younger vine',

Proud and stately again will it bloom
And silence all the past seasons' gloom.

Then, upon them, the sun will shine;
And, forever and always, on me and mine—

But, now, in night's silence in his empty room,
I give thanks to God—

My 'rose', still undaunted, blooms.

Marjorie E. Potter
December 15, 1970

With Us

Though you happen to be in another place,
You're here with us, for I see your face—

In the beautiful, dark eyes of your little son,
His walk, his talk, his smile so winsome,
In the light he brings to everyone—

Through the many kind deeds you've done for
      others,
The love you've given to your sister and brothers;
And, most of all, to your Father and Mother.

You perhaps didn't know, what happened to you
Brought us all closer together in a special way,
      too,
With new wisdom and judgment in all that we do.

You're with us now; and, you always will be—
In our hearts, and our faces for all to see.
Wherever we are, there, too, you'll be.

Our love for you spans all time and space,
Apart, or together, wherever the place—
You're here with us, for I see your face.

Marjorie E. Potter
December 23, 1970

The Voice Within

Sometimes I dream of what might have been,
If I hadn't listened to the 'voice within'—

Fond mem'ries, too—not barren and fallow,
What I felt for you was not flimsy and shallow—

But the highest regard, true love and devotion,
Not easy to handle that deep emotion.

And, some of those memories still linger to haunt me—
The 'voice within' that seemed to taunt me—

Whispered, shouted, murmured low,
And, finally sang to let me know

I could not leave and hope to gain
Lasting love, through others' pain.

Was it the voice of my higher self,
Teaching and guiding that other self,

Who wonders still what might have been,
If I hadn't listened to the 'voice within'?

Or, was it our fate to be denied
A love we neither could longer hide—

For mistakes we'd made in some other life?
Could you have taken another man's wife?

Could I have been the 'rejected lover',
Who, in this life, rejected another?

If this be true, then we can be certain,
That, again, before the 'final curtain',

The paths of our lives once more will entwine;
And, if you've paid your 'debt', and I've paid mine,

We'll cease to wonder what might have been,
If I hadn't listened to the 'voice within'.

Marjorie E. Potter
July 28, 1971

Lust

Every day, and every night,
Since just last week, when you walked out of
    sight,

I've thought of nothing else but you;
And, on your return, all we would do.

As, I had vowed in '67,
If chance arose, I'd sample 'heaven',

And, would have done so, when you were here,
Had not my fertile time been near—

The time you chose was inopportune,
Such are the vagaries of the moon.

I've dreamed of just how high I could fly,
On a sunlight hilltop, 'neath a clear blue sky—

Or, on a boat, out in the sound,
With no one else but the Captain around.

Or, here, most any afternoon,
While Babe's asleep, on the floor, I'd swoon!

Or, in the bathroom, for God's sake,
That moment of passion, I would take!

Or, the couch very quickly converts to a bed;
And, in your arms, inhibitions I'd shed,

Attaching no strings, no 'forever' vows,
To this clandestine affair of ours;

And, in later years, we'll have no regrets.
For the stolen moments we'll treasure yet,

When we open the pages of memory's book,
And, now and then, have a look

At the precious time we shared in life,
With no harm to my husband, and none to your
      wife;

But, now, we'll never know, I guess,
For, you're here in the East, and, I'm headed West.

Farewell, Dear Heart. it could have been great;
But, for now, I fear, it's just too late!

Marjorie E. Potter
July 30, 1971

The Doers' Society

Come, all productive people, in unison, rise up!
Let unproductive people know, our cup is now
      filled up!

And, tell your Representative,
In words he can't mistake,

The time has come for him to give
Attention to what's at stake.

A way of life we've all pursued,
While by the heads of state, we're wooed,

Lulled into a way of thinking
All's right with the world. Instead, it's sinking

Deeper and deeper into the trap
Of equalitarian 'clap-trap'.

Tell him to stop needless spending;
And, while we're at it, blatant lending.

We have 'had it' with this tax bite,
Which makes us, the Doers, fight

The burden of non-doers' plight—
Every morning, noon and night.

Now, the heads of state have faltered,
While states of man, they have altered,

With their ever-increasing efforts to bring
All mankind to the knees of one 'king'.

Just how long could their world keep spinning
Without the efforts of those who are winning?

Why should we keep on 'winning', I say,
When the government takes it all away?

So, winners, producers, all unite.
Show your muscle, and all your might.

Plan well ahead; and, all in one day,
Send one from among you to Washington to say—

"Mr. President, Sir, I'm here to announce
"That the Doers' Society wish to denounce

"This Government which has brought us to shame,
"Realizing we are, in part, to blame—

"We can put a stop to it,
"And, Sir, That's it! Right now—we quit!

"It'll do you no good to go to your phone,
"To call the Cabinet and wail and bemoan.

"The Doers are organized to a man
"And won't go back to work till there's a new plan.

"The trains won't run, the planes won't fly!
"Factories all over are on 'stand-by'.

"The farmers, the doctors, the steel mill hands,
"All kinds of workers, throughout the land,

"Are waiting now, prepared to stand strong
"And wait for the news, no matter how long,

"Till you and I together appear,
"From this news room, right over here—

"Oh, yes, Sir, they've all been alerted.
"It was necessary, you see, if crisis be averted

"Now, I know, you'll need some time to relax,
"Before you repeal the Income Tax!

"Don't worry, don't hurry, we're sure you'll
          agree—
"It's so much better than anarchy.

"May I remind you, Sir—We do have a plan
"To restore human dignity to each and every man.

"This tax repeal is just step number one;
"And, the Doers, as usual, will get the job done!"

Marjorie E. Potter
October 16, 1971

Legacy To My Children (And Others)

For the most part, I've been happy of heart,
And 'free' all my life, through problems and
      strife—

Tho' you can't really be completely 'free'
Of the pains of another, when you're called
      "Mother",

By several offspring, and the friends they bring
To your heart's door—my own number four.

We had our fears, through the early years,
With childhood diseases, and sniffles, and
      sneezes;

But, most of all, we had lots of fun,
And considered our job deserved a "Well done!"

And, now that the children are all quite grown,
I question: What kind of seeds have we sown?

For just when I think that we're on the brink
Of hoped-for success—here's another in a great
      big mess!

And, I wonder, at length, where I'll find the
      strength
To go on living—and giving, and giving.

Did I play some awful joke
For which I must yet bear a yoke

Of pain and sorrow too much to bear?
How could I have been so wrong, and where?

When were the 'twigs' so badly bent,
That love and affection don't make a dent—

In their hardened bark of hostility?
They can't seem to cope with reality.

My own past errors are not so dramatic
As to be to them completely traumatic:

But, no answers are clear,
As I write this here.

And, I've cried more tears than I care to recall.
I'm weary of crying, damn it all—

And, shouldering burdens for one and all.
At this stage of life, I should have a ball!

So, start fresh today with a brand new slate,
Get on with the business of 'making your fate'!

Stop blaming your elders for your inability
To face up to your responsibility.

Be true to yourself—
Don't sit on a shelf.

Leave the nest and do your best;
And, give your Mother and Dad a rest.

You're old enough now
To make a vow—

That whatever the problem you have to meet,
You'll face it squarely, on your own two feet!

I guess, my dears, that I've failed to convey,
That the 'game of life' is yours to play,

Not mine, not Dad's, or that of another's,
But, yours alone, excluding all others.

And, all my life, I've tried to do
Too much, to make it easier for you.

My strength has proved my 'Waterloo'—
Forgive, please, what that's done to you.

I'll listen still, if you've a need;
But, yours it is, to do the deed.

Epilogue

I'm really not satisfied with this ditty—
But it sums it all up in a manner witty!

Marjorie E. Potter
January 12, 1972

I Know

I think that now perhaps I know
The reason why one soul can grow
'Ere soaring high or creeping slow,
While yet another withers so...

What is the reason that one creates
The very trap he says he hates,
And dramatizes and berates
All others outside of his hell gates—?

What did he do that he felt so 'wrong'
As to hate himself so bitter and long
And compel all others to hear his song
Of woe and misery, all life long—?

Blaming others for his misdeeds—
Using others to fill his needs—
Seldom planting down good seeds—
Wondering why he plucks but weeds—?

If not his need to be proven right
By even one being within his sight,
That he'll go on trying with all his might
To justify his miserable plight.

If he but knew, he could be 'free',
By getting down on bended knee,
Confessing his 'mortal sin' to Thee,
O, God, Omnipotent— Let it be!

Then touch his heart and soul with yearning
To be of service and go on learning
With hope and faith and desire burning
To fulfill his mission for this 'returning';

And, let him earn a 'star in his crown'—
Put a smile on his face instead of a frown—
A light in his spirit to shine all around
And, let love in his heart for all abound.

This is my prayer, now that I know
That, in God's time, each soul can grow—
Early or late, fast or slow—
Never another need wither so.

Marjorie E. Potter
January 23, 1972

Musing—On New London

Oh, to be again in New London town,
And sit and watch the sun go down—

To wake each morn 'neath the Maple trees,
With my windows open to the breeze—

And bask in sunshine through the day,
Losing all thought of self for a day—

Reflecting on all the famous men
Who've walked these very streets; and, then,

Having lived out their lives, lie buried here.
History's here; and, with each year,

Becomes more and more inspiring.
Those now famous ones, never tiring,

Built a new world after the one they'd left,
Where man should never be bereft

Of the fruits of his labors, and all he'd earned...
This lesson was so sorely learned...

In self-respect, and, pride, if you will,
In all he'd done, whatever his skill.

I wonder—if they could come back today,
What these hardy men would have to say!

Would they say: "Get out of the war!"?
Or, would they all rally down at the shore;

And, man every ship, and hoist each sail—
Lashing a few fearful ones to the rail—

And prepare to defend what they'd hardly won—
Freedom from oppression, and rule by the gun...?

In this, our time, I'd like to believe
That these stout-hearted men would move to
      relieve

Any from office whose honor is in doubt!
They'd crank up their presses, and not fear to
      shout

Their considered opinions for all to hear—
"Our priceless freedom's at stake here!"

But. their voices, by death, long since are stilled...
Who among you is strong enough willed

To stir the people to treasure once more
The things that men died for on our own shore—?

The simple, basic human rights are no less sought
      today,
So, think, reason, and work for them—while you
      yet may.

Marjorie E. Potter
January 31, 1972

To A Friend

I'm sorry you've lost your dear friend.
It doesn't seem quite fair;
For, just as you'd started to live again,
He's gone—we know not where.

He's shed this body—that we know,
For quite a different kind;
And, for a time, perhaps he'll go
Where he'll find peace of mind.

But I'm convinced, he will return
To share again with you
The game of life—for he must yearn
For things he couldn't do.

He may decide to come back this year
In the birth of a child near you.
The love you shared while he was here
Must come again to you.

But, then again, he may wait it out,
For we're ever drawn by affinity—
That is what love is all about,
To be—throughout eternity.

So, cry for a bit, if you feel that way.
Let your tears wash away your sorrow—
For he is really just away.
And, you'll love him again some tomorrow.

Marjorie E. Potter
February 2, 1972

To Anne

This is my prayer for you, dear Anne,
To brighten your way somewhat, my friend.
It's my earnest desire to do what I can
There's a new beginning — 'tis not the end.

May the still, small voice within you
Always waiting to be heard,
Ease the grief and pain within you,
Give you strength with just a word.

As you keep your "quiet hour",
Once fondly shared with him,
May life's joys replace the sorrow
As that memory grows dim.

May you face each new tomorrow
With but happy thoughts of him;
And, in that 'quiet morning hour',
You'll share again with him.

Recall the pleasant moments;
And, his love will be with you.
Let memories flow to heart's content
To light your way and see you through...

And, the still, small voice within you,
Ever present to be heard,
Will relieve you of this burden
As you listen for the 'word'.

You asked me how I knew you'd found
The way to seek the 'Source'
And, the answer,
"I just knew", you'd found,
Is that each soul must, of course.

Marjorie E. Potter
July 15, 1972

Spirit Conversation

You've shed your body racked with pain,
And, now I know you're free;
But, yet, you've come back here again,
To share your time with me.

Please don't make me a vehicle
To give you life anew,
I'm past the age a babe to suckle,
Even to be with you.

'Twould be a different kind of love,
If Mother and Babe we'd be,
So, onward, Spirit, to heaven above;
And, wait up there for me—

Marjorie E. Potter
Summer, 1972

My Mailbox

Would that I could more often hear
From those far away, as well as those near.

Instead, the touters of goods of all kind
Keep mail coming in and are quick to remind

Me of bills coming due;
But, there's nothing from you.

And, my mailbox takes on an identity.....
It's either "friend" or "foe" to me.

On days when there's nothing there for me,
It's outright classed as: "Enemy"!

But, days when its contents make me merry,
It's no longer my adversary,

But a loving sentinel standing there
Receiving good news from those who care...

And, I vow I'll dress it in brand new paint
And bright bold letters in a style that is quaint,

With a separate section for bills coming due,
And one marked: "Special", for letters from you!

Marjorie E. Potter
September 10, 1972

To Cathy And Mary

Bless you for coming in time of need,
For every action, and every deed.

Like angels of mercy in answer to prayer—
At the darkest hour, you were suddenly there.

Woman needs man, we know that's true;
But, man needs woman for fulfillment, too.

While two of my sons suffered torments of hell—
At the mercy of women, who loved not well,

You appeared, as if called by God above,
To ease the pain, and fill them with love;

And, there's no end to what man can do,
For the love of a woman, just like you.

'Receivers', by nature, God made us to be;
But, we must give back, just as naturally—

For this makes man a 'receiver', too,
And balances God's gift of love for you.

Let no one judge you for being there,
For I know you came in answer to prayer.

God has a way for soul-mates to meet—
In a lonely room, or a crowded street—

In good times, or bad—in foul or fair weather,
And, He had a reason to bring you together.

Marjorie E. Potter
October 13, 1972

My Son

My son, happy youth, my son—
My son, young father, my son—
My son, grief stricken, my son—
My son, addicted, my son—
My son, imprisoned, my son—
My son, returning, my son—
—My son—

Inside the soul, what tortures dwell?
What motivates the man
To self-destruction—aye, to hell?
God, tell me if you can.

What dim guilt-laden memory
From what long distant past
Now drives him to this penalty?
God, how long must it last?

For overt acts, this life, he's paid,
Acknowledging his ways—
Knowing, his mistakes, he's made.
God, grant him bright new days.

If love be sick, then sick am I,
For love him still, I must;
Though, untold tears, I can't deny—
God, You, too, still love, I trust.

Somewhere, inside, there's pain repressed
For reasons he denies;
And, in this hell, it's all expressed.
God, straighten out the lies—

And grant him freedom from the pain
Of self-recrimination.
Show him the way out of the rain—
God, a brighter destination.

For he, too, is a 'Pilgrim God'
Who somehow got off course;
And, oh, the lowly trails he's trod,
God, filled with grief and remorse.

I place him in your trust and care—
Create his life anew.
With this, a Mother's heartfelt prayer
God, I give him now to You.

Marjorie E. Potter
November 14, 1972

It's Just A Thought Away

If you long to feel you're 'free' again—
To live life fully every day,
Just dream of what you might have been...
It's just a thought away!

For you can change the pattern—
Know who you are today...
Dream on, and take a different turn...
It's just a thought away!

For you're the master of the course
You choose in life today.
Waste not your time with grim remorse—
It's just a thought away!

No more self-recrimination
For mistakes of yesterday!
Seek bright, new destinations—
It's just a thought away!

So contemplate, within your mind,
New imagery each day;
And, peace and love, you'll surely find—
It's just a thought away.

Marjorie E. Potter
January 23, 1973

The Transition

I closed my eyes and saw the 'Light'—
God's own, approaching in the night;
And, offered up a silent prayer—
"Yes, come now, God, and take him there".

I thought about his earthly life—
Of joy and laughter, pain and strife—
The 'swallowed' pain—too much to bear—
His peace and love, a meager share.

He'd walked this life an earthy path,
Denied himself, and suffered wrath;
And, didn't know until too late,
He could be Master of his fate.

For a soul of greatness dwelt within;
And, when he'd recognized his 'sin'
Of daily dying, bit by bit,
He wanted to be 'done with it'!

What hopes and dreams now flood his mind
So fresh illumined and refined?
Does he still linger close at hand
To lend us all a helping hand?

I know I'll hear him sing his songs,
Forgive him for remembered 'wrongs'—
Love him, always, my own way;
And, pray for 'Light' for him each day.

As he goes now to the 'other life',
Free from pain, regret and strife.
I know he'll be with those held dear
On that other side, and yet, be here.

That boundless spirit now free at last
Won't dwell upon this earth life past;
But, rather, on what's yet to be,
As he lives on eternally.

Marjorie E. Potter
March 28, 1973

Life Begins At Forty

Life Begins at Forty, they say,
And, I'm just 'nine' years old—

I wonder: "What shall I do today—
Exactly as I am told?"

Ha! Ha! I've got a brand new life,
Stretched out in front of me.

Free of yesterday's cares and strife—
What a future it's gotta be!

Marjorie E. Potter
Spring, 1973

Revolt

My son thought up the ultimate revolt—
Don't go to the polls: don't cast a vote!

These people in office have got to retire
When their present terms just plain expire,

And those who are running to get elected
Will ask themselves why incumbents were
        rejected.

A team of honest citizens can then be hired
To see who remains, and who gets 'fired'!

And half the jobs will cease to exist;
But, we'll have good government if we persist.

No more pork-barrel, graft, or corruption
Just ethics, and justice and full production.

With this as our aim, it surely can be;
But, it all depends on you and me.

Marjorie E. Potter
May 9, 1973

Lord, Help Me!

Lord, help me to get through another day—
Help me to be a better 'Mother' to Clay,

As I am the only 'Mother' he's got;
And, whether he's mine; or, whether he's not,

I am the one to show him the way—
Thank you, Lord, for sending us Clay.

Give me the patience to allow him to 'be',
And not expect him to conform to me.

For he is a being of super strength;
And, I, too, must be—I've decided, at length;

Or, I wouldn't have this challenge before me,
If You didn't, indeed, absolutely adore me.

So, thank you, Lord, for giving me time
And the words and thoughts for praying this
      rhyme;

And, thanks again, for sending us Clay
And the blessings and tests he gives us each day.

Marjorie E. Potter
December 12, 1973

Touching

How would I know of your need to be touched
If I, too, didn't yearn to be touched?

How would I know of your need to see
If I, too, had no need to see?

How could I know of your need to hear the sound
    of my voice
Unless I, too, in yours rejoice.

The sounds of music, sadness and mirth
Reflect to me and give rebirth

To my own inner thoughts and needs—
Echoing all your moods and needs.

Could I perceive your need to taste
The tears that sometimes streak my face—

And smell my body close to you—
And yet not know they're my needs, too?

Because I think I understand
I offer you my 'touching' hands,

My 'seeing' eyes, and 'listening' ears—
My voice, responsive through all our years—

My sense of taste and smell to you
Because I know they're my needs, too.

Marjorie E. Potter
April 7, 1974

Encore

Finding out who I am has taken so long,
And I'm still not sure, as I write this song,

For as I travel along this life track,
I think many times of a long way back,

When I first really knew that life is a stage
upon which we, as players, engage,

And, then it was I decided to be
No longer, 'Reactor'; but, the 'Actor'—me!

And the 'play' that I'd already begun
Of right, had to be, 'Act Number 1'!

Of first importance, my family—
Getting them through to: 'Curtain, Act III',

So they could start their own new 'Play'
As they started off on their own way.

And, I'm still learning new roles to play,
Tho', at times, I may seem to lose the way—

I've just taken off for a short 'Intermission'
To gather my forces and check for remissions;

And, when I've tallied up the score,
I'll be back 'on stage' for a big 'Encore'.

So, if you're finding out who you really are—
Dream your big dreams—and wish on a star.

Don't be a 'Re-actor', but, the 'Actor', YOU!
And do all the things you want to do.

Marjorie E. Potter
December 31, 1974

The Poll

They didn't call me when they took the Poll;
And, I tend to resent the sweeping
    pronouncements
When Belding and Gallup make their
    announcements,
My name wasn't there when they called the 'roll'.

More often they're wrong than they've ever been
    right—
Yet their wordsmiths continue their game of
    semantics
The 'callers' contribute their part of the antics,
And I get so angry, sometimes, I could fight!

Let's un-do the scoundrels conducting the polls
And confound the wordsmiths and callers, too,
Next time they 'cross-section' me or you
And say to them: "Just leave my name off your
    rolls!"

"I'm not just a number with which you can toy—
Nor shall I be part of the game that you play,
As I quite disagree with the things that you say;
And I'm certainly not in your employ!"

"I'd think that by now you would have known,
You, Mind-benders, all, listen to me,
For I'll decide what's true to me,
As some of us here have minds of our own."

"I don't want to hear any more about it.
You'll have to contrive a much better game
If you think that you can use my name
For, I, for one, can do without it!"

Marjorie E. Potter
1975

Thoughts On New Year's Eve, '75

Now cry the tears you've left unshed
And wash away the torment

Of last year's tragic moments
Still fresh on memory's thread.

Add up those awful days gone by
And wipe them from the slate.

The New Year brings the chance to try
Again—It never is too late!

We'll paint a brighter canvas
Than the one of this year past,

Filled with thanks so we can have us
A New Year much better than the last.

Marjorie E. Potter
December 31, 1975

Feelings

The feelings I've so long suppressed
Return again to me,

Parading up and down undressed—
I don't like what I see.

I thought I had then all lined up
Like ten-pins in a row;

But, all I did was cover up,
So no one else would know

The anger and hostility,
The discontent and fears,

Frustrations and anxieties,
And all the unshed tears

Lay buried just below
 The surface of my consciousness,

Where no one else could go—
And I, alone, redress.

Marjorie E. Potter
April 1976

Another Life

Another life, another day,
We two, wandered this way,
Played in the sun in new fields of hay.
And, idled many hours away—

Chased the windswept leaves of fall,
Saw rainbows through 'our' waterfall,
Kissed raindrops from sudden showers,
Frolicked through the Springtime flowers—

Childhood playmates we then were—
Yet came to know love's first surrender—
Then beat the sound of distant drums,
Bidding all young warriors: "Come!"

And, lo, you went away,
Vowing you'd return
The day the battle had been won—
I watched you ride into the sun.

When fallen leaves again were thickening,
I felt the life within me 'quickening',
And waited calmly—trusting still,
I'd see you—riding—from 'our' hill.

The days grew short and winter's cold
Kept all secluded, save the bold...
And, then, Spring flowers broke the earth
My time had come for giving birth.

Hush! A rider, coming fast—
My sweet love coming home, at last—
I raised up from my mat of skin,
And saw a 'white' man riding in.

Fair haired he was, his eyes sky blue—
Yet, tan of skin and lithe, like you,
The white man who'd defended you,
And did his best to bring you through—

But, failing in his improbable task,
Had promised you he'd do as you asked.
He said he'd ridden far and wide,
To find me after you had died—

"Is this the camp where does abide
The fallen young brave's little bride?"
Your father gravely brought him to me,
My tear filled eyes could scarcely see—

He gave me first your amulet, and turquoise stone
    you wore.
I, half-believing, could not let this man speak to
    me more.
"No! No —— No!" Again I cried—
"These things all must be denied!"

Then, slowly, from his pouch he took
The brown square rock from 'our' special brook.
Then, back I fell, and all grew dim.
That was the last I saw of him.

Our son conceived in love's first bloom
Was born that night of solemn gloom.
I wakened later at day's first light,
The rock clutched in my hand throughout the
    night,

The rock that brought back all your love,
To hold me ever true;
And the Great White Spirit from up above,
Told me He was with you.

He told me, too, that I must be strong,
To walk with this Son his whole life long—
And, that I would die only when I grew old,
After this story had been many times told,

Of how you bravely fought and gave your life,
And left me, your little wife,
To bring this man-child to the fulfillment,
Of his destiny of great achievement—

That all men, 'white' and 'red' would come to
    understand,
That all could live in harmony on this, our land.
The birds were singing here in the wild—
Silently, I nursed our child.

The sunlight streamed into my birthing place—
And shone upon his little face,
And, I knew that he would grow to be
A very special honor, to you and me.

Marjorie E. Potter
December 5, 1977

The Sea

The sea, the sea,
The restless sea—

Always moving,
Constantly changing—

Goes far away,
And comes back to me,

Bringing me back
To reality.

I am a part of it;
And, it is a part of me.

Marjorie E. Potter
May 24, 1984

My Place

There's a trail that I know,
Where the wild flowers grow,

And a stream starts its way to the sea;
And, I like to go there,

And sit and stare,
In the shade of an old Oak tree.

Marjorie E. Potter
1985

I wrote this poem to help my Grandson, Clay, with a poem to translate into Spanish.

He got an "A"

This poem which follows is a poem message to my brother-in law, Eddie, who succumbed to prostate cancer in January 1986—in composition several days in August, 1985. I'd hoped beyond measure that I might be able to somehow work the 'magic' which would perhaps save his life— Perhaps it did extend it for some time.

Dear Eddie:

I'm sending you this little rock pet—
(I found him out on the beach!)
He can help you when you go to 'wet'.
If he's always within your reach.

All you do is gently rub him
When you take him into the 'john';
And believe that he will be your 'dub-in'
Every day from now on.

Keep him always close at hand
So he's right there to take your command.
Talk to him daily, and firmly say:
"Rocky, you take the cancer away!"

Tho' you may not believe in runestones 'n' such,
You'll surely agree that it can't hurt much.
So why not give it a try anyway,
And repeat the words each and every day!

For who knows how the body heals
Or, for all that, how a cancer 'feels'?
Or, maybe after all, there is 'someone' there
To hear the words that we declare.

We see with our eyes that healing occurs,
When it's anywhere on our skin.
But, oh, how swiftly our vision blurs,
When we have to look within.

This is not much as a little verse,
But it gets the point across—
If you're gonna put this thing in 'reverse',
You gotta remember who's 'Boss'!

Love you, always,

Marge

Marjorie E. Potter
1985

Miss You

Not a day goes by
That I don't cry
For you;

And, no matter how I try,
I just can't help but cry,
For you.

I'd give everything I own
Or ever hope to own,
If I could give you life anew.

If I could take away the pain,
And make you whole again,
That's all I'd ever want to do.

I miss you, I miss you, I miss you,
Miss you, miss you, miss you,
Miss you——

Marjorie E. Potter
Spring '1994

Dear Ones: This is the song I 'cried' for your dad, my Johnny, written on the way to Spicewood/Bertram in early '94, as best I can remember now. Just out of San Antonio on north highway 281, I started 'crying it out' and somewhere between north San Antonio and Johnson City or Blanco, I 'hen-scratched' the dots to represent notes and the lyrics as I drove along, so that I wouldn't forget it. (dangerous).

I sang it for each of you, as I seemed compelled to do, on separate occasions and could barely do it, and you could hardly stand to hear me do it. I'm sorry.

The date of this writing is May 16, 2000. It's been nearly seven years since he died, and I still cry as I write it here, or if I try to sing it. Wherever else I have it 'written' down, I don't remember, but I thought I should put it here.

Now, if I just had a Music Program, I could write the score here, too. I may try.

Miss You (The Song)

Not a day goes by
  C   D   F   E   E
That I don't cry
   D   E   F   D
For you;
  C   D

And, no matter how I try,
   D   E   F G   F   E F
I just can't help but cry,
G E   F   E   D   E
For you
  C   E

I'd give everything I own
  E   F   G A   F   G
Or ever hope to own
  E   G A   G   F   G
If I could give you life anew.
F G   A   F   E   E   D E

If I could take away the pain,
C C   D   E   F E   D   E
And make you whole again,
  F   D   E   D   C E
That's all I'd ever want to do
   G   D E D E   F   B C

I miss you, I miss you, I miss you,
G F   E   C A   G   G F   E
Miss you, miss you, miss you,
 D   C   D   C   D   C
Miss you --- ---
  F   E

I tried with just my ear --- no keyboard --- to record
The notes of the song. Someday I'll try to check it
Against a keyboard.

There may be errors in these "notes".

Marjorie E. Potter
May 16, 2000

If A Thief You Be

Welcome, Pal,
If a thief you be,

Door's open—
Come right in on me!

Come on in and steal me blind,
If that is what you have in mind.

Be careful you don't leave behind
Fingerprints for the cops to find—

Your photo, too, for all to see
Is recorded here now, for posterity.

So, onward, Pal, if you really do dare,
Take everything I have—I just don't care!

Sooner or later, you will be caught;
And, all your efforts will be for naught.

Better have lots of money to make your bail,
'Cause you surely are going to end up in jail!

Marjorie E. Potter
August 16, 2000

To My First Love

Oh, how I loved you
All those many years ago!
I thought that my whole life was through
When my folks said: "He has to go!"

I faltered for a little while;
But, then, went 'onward with a smile'.
I met a new love,
And, so did you.

As we matured and each nurtured
The new lives in our hands,
From dawn 'til dark, our days were filled
With the children's many demands.

But, as they grew and left the nest,
We found new things to do;
And, 'Father Time' said: "Time to rest!"
Now—what do we do?

The 'Golden Years' are here at last—
And, as we reflect on days gone by,
We wonder how time flew so fast.
Where did it go—And Why?

Recapture if we could—we would
Our youth and love's first bloom;
And relive all the happy times when we were such
      a team;
But, age again denies us—everything but the
      dream.

So far apart our paths have been
A continent apart—
And, yet, when we're together again.
That love still swells my heart.

I love you as I did before,
And, sadly, miss you, too—
And, knowing that you still love me more
Makes everything seem 'new'!

There could still be a special time
Just for you and me—
Remembering the words of this very special
      rhyme,
May make it our true destiny.

——Love you——!

Marjorie E. Potter
October 14, 2000

Time

Time is the Arbiter,
No barriers knows He

But that he will
Simply always BE!

Marjorie E. Potter
October 16, 2000

When I Grow Old

I've been thinkin' 'bout some things I'll do,
If I want to—when I grow old.
Maybe I'll just sit and stare in a rockin' chair—
Not goin' anywhere...

Or, watch a spider spin a web,
With its endless, tireless spinning,
Up and down, back and forth,
Without end—and no beginning.

Then, maybe, I'll just rock and think.
Perhaps I'll take a little drink
Of Elderberry Wine. That's so fine—
If I really want to—when I grow old.

And, I shall wear pink—and green—
and purple—and ORANGE—
All together, of course,
If I want to—when I grow old.

Maybe I'll dance around the house, naked as a
 Jaybird! Who's to care?
And then, I'll don a pretty gown—and pretend I'm
Ginger Rogers, Dancin' with Fred Astaire, or
 Nureyev, Chevalier, Youskevitch or Kelley,
If I want to—when I grow old.

And, then, I'll pretend I'm a great entertainer,
Singing my heart out—
And taking my bows to thunderous applause,
And people shouting: "Encore! Encore! Encore!"

Again, perhaps I'll sit and stare in my rocking
    chair,
Hands folded neatly in my lap,
While I take time out for a little nap,
If I want to—when I grow old.

And, will my hair ever turn white;
Or, will I still be putting up a fight
To hide the graying roots and add a bit of gold,
If I want to—when I grow old?

And, can't I fantasize about making love with a
    gentle lover
Who sees me still as young and vibrant—
Even knowing I'm growing old—
If I want to—when I grow old?

And, I'll melt in his arms, responding to his
    passionate kisses with plenty of my own—
And we'll stay in our special trysting place, as
    long as we want to;
And, live and laugh and love, forever!
If I want to—when I grow old.

Marjorie E. Potter
June 5, 2002

Words

Pardon Me! May I have your attention, please?
This is a poem about words, and I must have your
undivided attention. And, I do thank you.
See? How I 'touched' you — merely with my
    words?

WORDS are power. WORDS are a gift.
WORDS can command, and demand and get
    results!
WORDS have the power to move you...
To laughter — to purest joy;
To tears and the deepest sorrow;
To the very heights of exhilaration and
    expectation
Or, the depths of despair...

Words can sear, scorch, scar scathe -
Or, soothe, soften, sweeten and swell the heart.

WORDS can thrill; or, words can kill the spirit
And dash all hopes and dreams; and, all is lost.
All is nothingness, emptiness — hopelessness.

WORDS can elevate, enlighten and inspire the
    searching soul
To unlimited greatness,
as the human spirit quite naturally soars
And aspires to achieve the ultimate beauty,
Whether in Architecture, Music, Art or Poetry.

Our beautiful language is truly a gift;
And ours it is to choose most carefully the words
    we use.
We can give the gift of Love, Forgiveness,
    Tenderness, Kindness,
Thoughtfulness, Compassion and
    Understanding—all universal solvents;

And, we can observe immediate results in kind.

What a wonderfully different world we can create
    — all with WORDS.

Marjorie E. Potter
2006

Wouldn't You?

If I could not walk,
You'd try to help me, wouldn't you?

If I could not speak,
You'd get me pen and paper, wouldn't you?

If I could not see,
You'd gently lead me, wouldn't you?

If I could not feel your loving touch,
You'd completely enfold me in your arms,
      wouldn't you?

If I could not hear
You'd get me pen and paper again, wouldn't you?

Because to each of us, our senses are so vital,
I give you pause to ponder these thoughts.

Marjorie E. Potter
October 6, 2007

If We Could But See Tomorrow

If we could but 'see' tomorrow,
What might we change today?
Would we be 'looking back' in sorrow,
For things we failed to do or say?

For failing to tell a loved one,
By some kind word or deed,
That whatever the 'slight', whether imagined or
    true,
Our love is constant, no matter what they do—

Would we wish we'd said: "I'm sorry",
To a loved one who just 'slipped away';
And, now, can never hear our apology?
What would we, if could we, say?

God doesn't give any guarantee,
When He assembles our family tree.
We must accept each other, whatever the
    challenge may be—
And this is true for all of us, even you and me.

Marjorie E. Potter
May 15, 2009

Forgiveness is profound in its ability to heal—not only the forgiven, but also the one who forgives. As they say:

"To err is human: to forgive is Divine". Alexander Pope, an English Poet and Satirist, who lived 1688-1744. He also said:

"And, all who told it added something new—
And all who heard it made enlargements, too".
Very interesting—and so long ago.

About The Author

Marjorie E. Potter, (Marge) is a Licensed Real Estate Broker, now retired. "Encore" is her first book. She has been member of the International Society of Poets, now published at www.Poetry.com, and was a member of the Harlingen Board of REALTORS, the Texas Association of REALTORS, and the National Association of REALTORS, the Rotary Club of West Cameron County, the I.A.A.P.A., (International Association of Amusement Parks and Attractions). Prior to her career in real estate, while living in Austin, Texas where she raised her four children with her husband of 49 years, Johnny Potter, she was a member of the Austin Civic Theatre, now the Zachary Scott Theatre, served on the Board of Directors, and was nominated for Best Supporting Actress of the Year for her portrayal of 'Mammy Yoakum' in the Show, "Li'l Abner" by Al Capp, a production in which all four her children, Travis, Jerry, Karen and Todd performed. She played in several productions including "Gypsy", acted as co-director for one show and loaned her strong musical voice to others even when not 'on stage'.

A graduate of Stockbridge Valley High School in Munnsville, New York, where she grew up on a farm and attended a two room school house, (grades two through six), Marge left New York for the West where she lived with her maternal Grandparents for nearly a year and worked for United States Steel subsidiaries while they were building the great steel plant in Provo, Utah. In the heat of patriotic fervor, and the height of World War II, she enlisted in the AIR W.A.C.S. It was during her tour of duty in Atlantic City, N. J. that she met and married her Texan, T/Sgt. John T. Potter, of Austin, Texas. When the war in Europe ended in May of 1945, then President Truman moved to discharge some military personnel to bolster morale back home, and her 'Johnny' was 'top point' man at A.A.F.R.S. #1, (The United States Army Air Force Redistribution Station #1), having been wounded flying combat as an Engineer/Gunner on a B-17 out of North Africa, and having been awarded the Purple Heart, The Distinguished Flying Cross, and the Air Medal with ten Oak Leaf Clusters, all of which added up 'points' for discharge; and, suddenly, they were homeward bound for Texas with a brand new baby boy.

After her fourth child was born, she attended Nixon Clay Commercial College, graduating in 1951; and, beginning with her first session of the Texas Legislature in 1951, she worked every session through 1965. She was first licensed as a Real Estate Agent in 1963, just before the Kennedy Assassination. She quit Real Estate in 1967 to spend more time with her family, re-emerging like the Phoenix in 1977, with a voracious zeal for attaining her goal of becoming a Broker.

Moving to the Rio Grande Valley in 1980, Marge soon established her own home office, Potter Properties, which she operated until 2014. With a heavy heart, she discontinued her real estate activities to leave her home in Harlingen of over 30 years to relocate to the Hill Country of Texas to be closer to some of her children, grandchildren, great grandchildren and her niece and nephew.

Marge has traveled widely, even to Scotland where her daughter was married in an ancient Castle, and to the Great Wall of China as a Member of a select delegation from I.A.A.P.A. through the auspices of the People to People International Citizens' Ambassador Program. At this printing, Marge boasts with pride that she has five grandchildren, seven great-grandchildren and one great-great grandson

www.ingramcontent.com/pod-product-compliance
Lightning Source LLC
Chambersburg PA
CBHW050041080526
44586CB00014B/1409